BIBLE INSIGHTS: BIBLE BOOK STUDIES FOR YOUTH

EPHESIANS

The Winning Team

By Thomas Couser

CPH™
SAINT LOUIS

Editor: Thomas A. Nummela

Editorial assistant: Phoebe W. Wellman

We solicit your comments and suggestions concerning this material. Please write to Product Manager, Youth and Adult Bible Studies, Concordia Publishing House, 3558 S. Jefferson Avenue, St. Louis, MO 63118-3968.

1 2 3 4 5 6 7 8 9 10   03 02 01 00 99 98 97 96 95 94

Contents

Welcome to Bible Insights!

Welcome to the Bible Insights series of Bible studies for youth! These materials are designed to provide study opportunities that explore selected books of the Bible in depth and apply the wisdom these books impart to the real-life issues young people face every day. Each book in this series has been carefully prepared to speak to the needs and concerns of youth, providing insight from God's Word. Each book consists of four sessions of study. Each can be used for weekly Bible study or selected studies can be used alone. The books can also form the core material for a Bible-study retreat or seminar.

This book is designed for the leader of the sessions. It provides all the information and instructions necessary for an effective Bible study. Each chapter concludes with several pages you can reproduce for the students in your group. Additional background information on the Bible book to be studied and some helpful information about small-group Bible studies are included in the Introduction.

May God bless your study by the Spirit's power, as you lead young people to greater insight about God's Word and the good things God desires to bring through it to their lives.

Introduction

About This Course

Course Objectives

Ephesians: The Winning Team, tells you a little about this study. Obviously, the basis for our study will be St. Paul's letter to the Ephesians. In this letter Paul coaches the Ephesian church and offers affirmation and spiritual guidance to them and to us. Through this study the following truths should become clear:

1. God desires that all people receive His blessings—forgiveness of sins and life eternal—through faith in Jesus Christ as their personal Savior.

2. God makes this possible as He invites all of us to become members of His team.

3. God also gives each of us particular gifts that can be used to serve others and to benefit the team.

Building Relationships

The mission effort among the Ephesians was successful in part because the Christians in that city related to and supported each other. Promote the same qualities with your youth Bible class.

Teenagers live in a "put down" culture. Even among friends they feel the pressure to give people degrading nicknames or to tease them in other ways. While some of this is done without intending harm, the end result can often damage the self-image of the recipient. Young people long for acceptance. They want others to accept them for who they are.

The relationships between your students are a primary dynamic in any youth Bible class. These relationships are one of the principal reasons young people come together. They can be a tool you use to increase their enjoyment and their learning during the study sessions. Most sessions call for spending some time in small groups of three to five students. These small-group times allow individuals to express their faith, respond to challenging questions, and participate in a low-threat environment. They can be very productive times. Make the most of them.

Who Are the Ephesians?

During his third missionary journey Paul stayed for three years in the city of Ephesus in Asia Minor. The reason for the extended visit was threefold.

1. Believers provided him with a support system.
2. In many respects, Paul had an ideal setting to carry out his min-

istry. Initially, Paul taught in the synagogue, but the Jewish leaders, threatened by his message, banned him; so Paul found a new forum in the hall of Tyrannus. The apostle most likely rented the lecture hall in the afternoons, a less desirable time because of the mid-day heat. The arrangement worked for Paul, however, since it allowed him to pursue his vocation as a tentmaker during the morning.

3. Lastly, Paul found his ministry to the Ephesians challenging since Ephesus was the "capital city" for several pagan religions.

Ephesus was located three miles from the Aegean Sea. It was a great commercial center. It was also the home to a wide collection of exorcists, magicians, cultists, and religious prostitutes. The immoral activities of the city probably offended Paul, but also commanded his attention.

The major tourist attraction in Ephesus was the statue to Artemis (Diana). People flocked to the city to view and worship the goddess. The presence of such an attraction encouraged a number of entrepreneurs, who made replicas of the statue and sold them at a profit. Paul's teachings about the one true God brought him into direct conflict with these businessmen. One of them, Demetrius, led the opposition. His concern was that the presence and teachings of Paul and his associates threatened the economy of the city. The end result was the riot recorded in **Acts 19.** Paul and his followers were able to escape, but the event brought their personal ministry in Ephesus to a halt.

The seeds of faith that Paul had planted, however, took root. The church in Ephesus grew. Perhaps it was due to Paul's extended stay or the close relationship he established with the people. The Christians in Ephesus had a deep affection for Paul. The emotion displayed during his final visit with the elders from Ephesus prior to returning to Jerusalem **(Acts 20:17–28)** demonstrates that. Paul's relationship with the Ephesians was distinctive when compared to other churches he planted.

The Letter to the Ephesians

Ephesians is one of the "captivity" letters, written during Paul's imprisonment in Rome.

This letter stands out since it addresses the mission of the church and the important role of each individual in that mission.

Paul As the Author

That Paul visited Ephesus during his missionary journey, and that he personally addresses the letter **(Eph. 1:1)**, point to him as the author. The writing also is consistent with Paul's style. In addition, many of the concepts presented in other Pauline epistles appear also in Ephesians: the body of Christ **(4:16)**, the temple of God **(2:20–22)**, and the church as the bride of Christ **(5:23–32)**.

Paul had a strong commitment to people, particularly to the people with whom he had shared his faith in Jesus. His relationship with those he brought to the faith was second only to his relationship with Christ.

While Paul was writing to the first-century church, the concepts as they apply to faith and discipleship are still relevant.

Building the Team

Each of the four lessons uses the concept of a basketball team. Participants have the opportunity to select players for the team, evaluate their fellow players, and react to certain situations that take place during the team's season.

The team concept, as it is presented, does not require any past interest or knowledge of the game of basketball. It is used only to relate the fact that God chose us all for His team. God gives us unique gifts and talents so that we can make a contribution toward the success of the team—the growth of His kingdom.

You could further promote the concept by encouraging the class to select a team mascot or develop a class logo. Add the mascot or logo to T-shirts or caps. The classroom could be decorated like a school hallway on the week before a big game, with signs and posters encouraging and supporting the team. To further enhance the team concept, a page of team cheers is included on Student Page 5. You could use them to open or close class sessions.

Nobody knows the needs of your students like you do. Every class is different. Each individual has specific and different needs.

With that in mind, this course is written with lots of options. There is more material here than you can use. You can select the activities that fit the needs of your class and your style.

Have Fun As You Learn

Teenagers have a genuine desire to deal with life's tough issues. In addition, Christian teens yearn to grow in their knowledge of God and His Word as they live as His disciples.

Today's youth also enjoy having fun. Strive early in the course to establish a casual, relaxed style. Teens also live in a dynamic and fast-paced world. Plan activities that last no more than 10–15 minutes. Have optional or additional activities ready for groups or individuals who finish the task ahead of time.

Plan Ahead

With some advance planning, you will be able to greatly enhance the effectiveness of this course. Begin scanning the sport section of your local newspaper to find articles that deal with motivation and values in athletics. Sport magazines will also be a good source. If there is a local chapter of the Fellowship of Christian Athletes, it can provide additional resources.

If your classroom does not have a chalkboard, you will benefit from a pad of newsprint. It is usually available from an office-supply or art-supply store.

Music is an important part of the life of teenagers. You might consider using one of the following songs as a theme song for the course: "Was It Worth It?" by Don Wharton, from the album *Pull Together* (available from Third Firkin Music by calling 615/865-1890) or "Destined to Win" by Degarmo and Key, available through most Christian bookstores.

Other activities or resources that might take advance planning include the following:

In session 1, the Tom Rogers' video is available from Lutheran Visuals, P.O. Box 550397, Dallas TX 75355, 1-800-527-3211.

In session 2, *Baptism: Sacrament of Belonging* is available in 16mm film or in video from Mass Media Ministries, 2116 N. Charles, Baltimore, MD 21218. Some Districts also have this item in their media libraries.

Small Groups Are Key

Setting Up the Groups

If your class on a regular basis has more than five students, it is best to divide them into small groups. The ideal group size is from three to five students. Continuity will be enhanced if you maintain the same groups throughout the course.

How the groups are formed is up to you. The easiest way is to allow the participants to form their own groups. That does not encourage the participants to establish new friendships, however. A better method might be to randomly place the students into groups. The determining factor is up to you. You could cluster students around birthdays (those born in January and February working together) or color of clothes (those wearing the most blue work together). Another fun way might be to have the students convert all the digits in their street address to a single number. For example 292 North 1st Street becomes 2921. In a class of eight students, the four highest and the four lowest numbers would work together.

The Small-Group Advantage

Some youth might initially resist the idea of working in a small group. They perhaps feel it denies them the opportunity to work with special friends. Yet the end result can often be beneficial. The reality is that most people relate better in a small group.

- Friendships are more easily established.
- It is also easy to share opinions and feelings.
- It also takes less effort to move new people into small groups than into larger ones. Newcomers will feel more comfortable entering into a group of 4, as opposed to a group of 20.

The Empty Chair

To ease the process of welcoming new people into small groups you might encourage participants to use the empty chair. Every small group should have at least one extra chair that is left vacant. That chair is available for the next person who enters the group. When that chair becomes occupied an additional chair is added.

Encourage group members to work at filling the empty chair. Encourage them to invite unchurched friends or friends who have become inactive. Allow those who bring friends to have them in the same small group, at least for the duration of this course.

The empty chair can become a way to encourage growth and openness to change.

Congratulations, You're on the Team!

(Eph. 1:15–2:10)

Where We're Heading

At times we all experience bitterness after not making a team. It is hard to go through such an event and not feel a lack of acceptance. In God's kingdom we have all made the team. We are all "first-round draft picks" by God, who through Christ chose each of us to be member of His team.

Objectives

By the end of this session, the participants will be able to
1. confess their failure to make God's team by their own abilities;
2. rejoice that God has chosen them for His team through Christ;
3. give thanks for the "riches of grace" **(Eph. 2:7)**, which they have received.

Materials Needed

- Bibles
- Pencils
- Copies of Student Pages 1–5
- Markers and paper

Bible Study Outline: Congratulations, You're on the Team!

Activity	Minutes	Materials Needed
Introductory Activity	5	Student Page 1
Imitators of Christ	10	Student Page 2 (Activity Cards)
Dateline Ephesus	10	Student Page 1, Bibles, paper
Who Will Make the Team?	15	Student Page 3
Making God's Team	15	Student Page 4, Bibles
The Good News: You Still Make the Team	10	Student Page 4, Bibles
Closing Activity	5	Student Page 5

As the Students Arrive

Greet class members as they arrive. Mount Student Page 1 (a–d) in a place where all can see it.

Prior to the session make a copy of Student Page 2, Imitators of Christ. Cut the sheet along the dotted lines to make activity cards. Recruit several students and give them one or more of the activity cards. Most of the activity cards require two students to work together. Assign them to plan a pantomime that illustrates the event. Encourage them not to share the information on their activity card(s) with anyone.

Introductory Activity

Call the class together. Begin the session with a prayer such as the following: "Gracious Father, we thank You for the opportunity to be together today. We are grateful that You have made us members of Your team. Bless our study today. Help us to better understand Your desires for us. Amen."

Briefly discuss Paul's missionary journeys and his work with the Ephesians. Use Student Page 1 (a–d) to focus on the unique challenges that Ephesus presented Paul as he sought to spread the Gospel (see Introduction).

Imitators of Christ

Inform the class that Paul challenged the Ephesians to be imitators of Christ. Jesus has given us specific examples of what it means to be His disciples, imitators of Him. Have each volunteer present a pantomime of the event listed on the activity card they received. Jesus demonstrated His servanthood in each. Have class members raise their hands when they think they have discovered the event being pantomimed. Allow the presenter at least 15 seconds to act out the event. Then call on the individual who had first raised his or her hand.

Dateline: Ephesus

Refer the students again to Student Page 1. Review the background information provided in the Introduction. Read about Paul's experience in Ephesus recorded in **Acts 19.** Ask the students to write brief news articles on the events that took place in Ephesus during Paul's visit. Use the map and Scripture passage as resources. Possible headlines include, "Jewish Evangelist Begins New Crusade in Hall of Tyrannus" or "Local Merchants View Evangelist as Reason for Sales Decline."

Who Will Make the Team?

Divide your class into small groups of three to five students.

Assign each group the task to select six players (five starters and one substitute) for a girls basketball team. Distribute Student Page 3, "Who

Will Make the Team?" Give the groups no more than five minutes to complete the task.

When you sense that all groups have completed the assignment, call the class together. Discuss briefly the way they approached their task. How did they decide which girls would make the team? What qualities did they look for? Why did they select certain players and not others? Were all the players equally talented? Who would they select as captain of this fictional team?

Discuss with the class the feelings that come from not making a team. Invite class members to share times when they have failed to make a team. Ask the groups to write brief letters to the girls who did not make the team. Remind them to be positive in their comments and to encourage the girls to use the gifts that God has given them in other ways. Invite one or more groups to share their letters.

Remind participants that success in athletics might be important in human terms but success in God's kingdom is much more important. Encourage the class to seek role models who demonstrate discipleship.

Making God's Team

Remind the class that Paul called the Ephesians to be imitators of Christ. He wanted them to be part of God's team. Throughout his letter Paul speaks of the characteristics needed to be a member of God's team.

Tell the students that the next activity is intended to help them evaluate their ability to perform well as a member of God's team.

Distribute copies of Student Page 4, "The Qualities Needed for Making God's Team." Instruct the class members to work individually on the sheet. Encourage them to read the Scripture references so that they have insight into Paul's request and God's desire.

At the end of the activity students will need to consult **Eph. 2:1–5** to discover the harsh reality when it comes to our ability to make God's team. Instruct them to use the space provided to record their discovery.

After 10 minutes, or when you sense that all have completed the assignment, call the class together. Question the students on their reaction to the first part of the activity. How do they feel about their ability to make God's team? What qualities do they possess? What qualities do they lack?

Review the characteristics. Why are each important? The comments that follow will assist you.

• Wisdom—knowing what God desires for us

• Revelation—acknowledging that God is the one who makes it possible for us to be on the team in the first place

• Love—agape: demonstrating the sacrificial love of Christ

• Power—having the ability to do God's will in even the most difficult situations

• Readiness—being aware of life situations as they develop so that we can at all times react in a Christ-like manner

Ask one or more students to share the harsh reality they discovered in **Eph. 2:1–5.** No one is good enough for God's team!

13

The Good News: You Still Make the Team!

Ask for a volunteer to read aloud **Eph. 2:4b–7.** Then ask the following questions: "What is the Good News? How did God make it possible for us to be on His team?"

Direct the students to return to their small groups. Instruct them to complete their review of this section of Ephesians by reading together **Eph. 2:8–10.**

Provide each group with paper and markers. Then instruct them to develop a motivational slogan based on the principles discovered in this section. The slogan should be similar to the ones that hang in team locker rooms but appropriate for motivating the members of God's team. Possible slogans: "Jesus Made You What You Are" or "God Gave You the Gifts; the Coach Gives You the Opportunity." Mount the slogans on the wall for all to see. At the conclusion of the activity, allow each group to share their slogan.

Closing Activity

Use one of the cheers on Student Page 5.

Conclude the session with a prayer such as the following: "Loving Father, thank You for the wonderful gift of Your Son, Jesus. Thank You too for making it possible for us to be part of Your team through His work on our behalf. Now, make us worthy team members. Help us to live our lives sacrificially for Jesus' sake, using all our gifts and abilities to serve You and others in His name. Amen."

Follow-Up Activities

Team Cheers

The class might have fun learning the cheers and working them into a routine. Simple dance steps or cheerleader-style actions could be developed to accompany the cheers. Use class members who have cheerleading experience as a resource. Or have the class develop their own cheers. Consider videotaping the cheers to share with others. Such tapes might become great promotional tools for recruiting new members to join your class or youth group.

Tom Rogers Video

At the 1992 National Lutheran Youth Gathering, "A Time for Joy!" held in New Orleans, Pastor Tom Rogers told a dramatic story. The incident is a good example of how God can recruit even the least obvious people to be part of His team. The video is available from Lutheran Visuals, P.O. Box 550397, Dallas, TX 75355, 1-800-527-3211. The video would make an excellent follow-up activity, either in class or at a future youth event.

Paul's Missionary Journeys

The First Journey (c. A.D. 46–48)
Acts 13:4–14:28

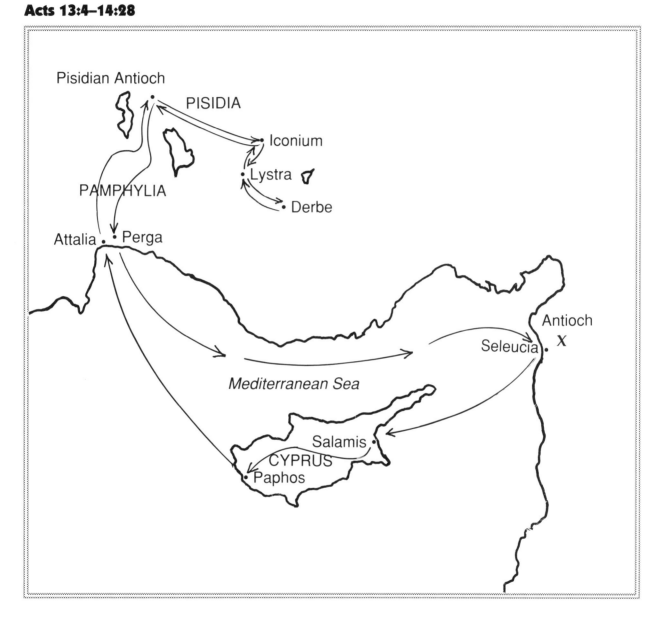

Pisidian Antioch

PISIDIA

Iconium

Lystra

Derbe

PAMPHYLIA

Attalia · Perga

Antioch

X

Seleucia

Mediterranean Sea

Salamis

CYPRUS

Paphos

Ephesians, Student Page 1A

Paul's Missionary Journeys—Continued

The Second Journey (c. A.D. 49–52)
Acts 15:39–18:22

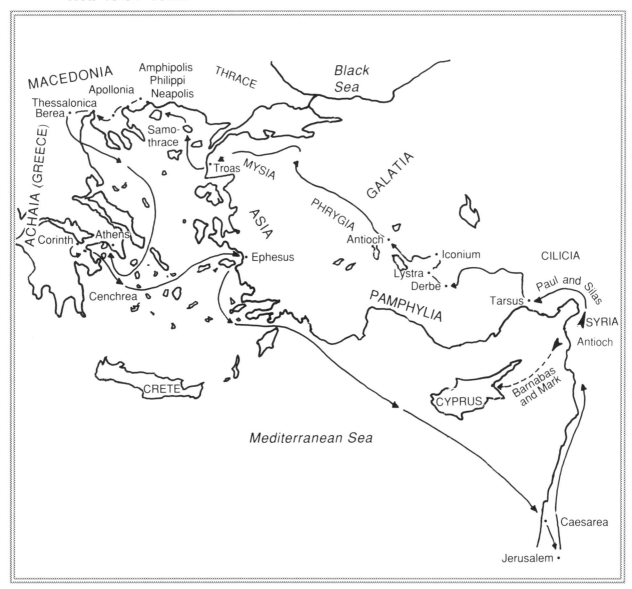

Paul's Missionary Journeys—Continued

The Third Journey (c. A.D. 53–57)
Acts 18:23–21:17

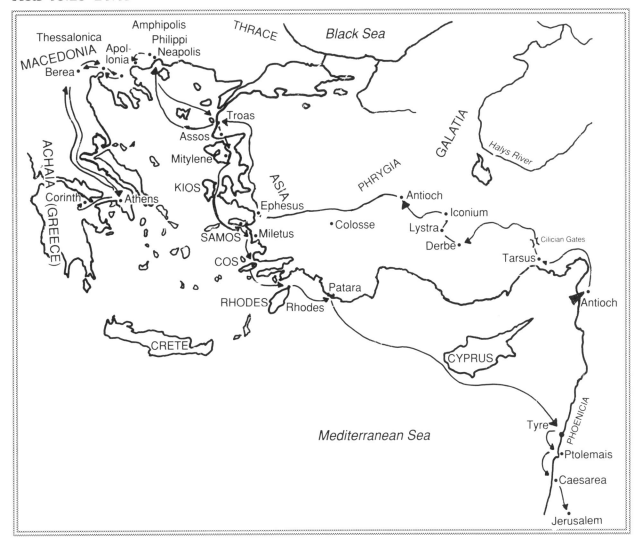

Ephesians, Student Page 1C

Paul's Missionary Journeys—Continued

The Journey to Rome (c. A.D. 59–60)
Acts 27:1–28:16

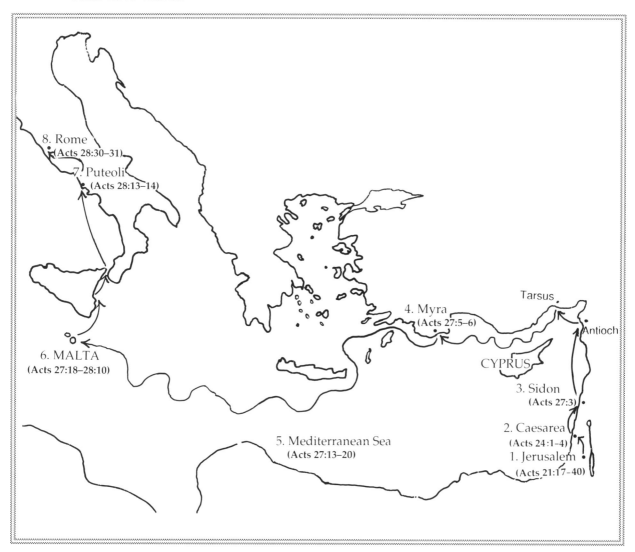

8. Rome
(Acts 28:30–31)

7. Puteoli
(Acts 28:13–14)

4. Myra
(Acts 27:5–6)

Tarsus

Antioch

6. MALTA
(Acts 27:18–28:10)

CYPRUS

3. Sidon
(Acts 27:3)

2. Caesarea
(Acts 24:1-4)

5. Mediterranean Sea
(Acts 27:13–20)

1. Jerusalem
(Acts 21:17–40)

Ephesians, Student Page 1D © 1994 CPH

Imitators of Christ

1. Jesus heals the blind man.

2. Jesus washes the disciples' feet.

3. Jesus walks on water.

4. Jesus stills the storm.

5. The boy Jesus listens to teachers in the temple.

6. Jesus is tempted by the devil.

7. Jesus kicks the money changers out of the temple.

8. Jesus is tried and crucified.

9. Jesus is resurrected from the grave.

10. Jesus calls the disciples. ("I'll make you fishers of men.")

Who Will Make the Team?

You must select six (five starters and one substitute) from the players below.

Rhonda
Characteristics: Tall, strong, good rebounder, average shooter

❏ Starter ❏ Sub ❏ Cut

Beth
Characteristics: Short, strong, only average speed, good defense, poor shooter

❏ Starter ❏ Sub ❏ Cut

Huwon
Characteristics: Short, very quick, aggressive, good outside shot

❏ Starter ❏ Sub ❏ Cut

Tico
Characteristics: Excellent short-range shot, aggressive, tends to foul

❏ Starter ❏ Sub ❏ Cut

Sheena
Characteristics: Tall, good inside shot; has a heart defect that only allows play for short spurts at a time

❏ Starter ❏ Sub ❏ Cut

Ephesians, Student Page 3A © 1994 CPH

Gwen
Characteristics: quick thinker, weak and slow, caring person/thinks of others first, good shooter

❏ Starter   ❏ Sub   ❏ Cut

Kara
Characteristics: Tall, good rebounder, slow because of physical defect, average shot

❏ Starter   ❏ Sub   ❏ Cut

Tina
Characteristics: Good athlete, good ball handler, tends to want to do everything herself

❏ Starter   ❏ Sub   ❏ Cut

Cindy
Characteristic: Likable person, somewhat slow, average shot, learning disability

❏ Starter   ❏ Sub   ❏ Cut

The Qualities Needed for Making God's Team

Reference	Characteristic	Description	Yes	No
Eph. 1:15	Love	Unselfishness: putting others first		
Eph. 1:17	Wisdom	Insight: knowing the rules (God's desires)		
Eph. 1:17	Revelation	Good Perspective: pure knowledge of God		
Eph. 6:10	Power	Strength: doing God's will in all situations		
Eph. 6:15	Readiness	Agility: the ability to react quickly		

The Harsh Reality:

See **Ephesians 2:1–5** to discover the harsh reality when it comes to our ability to make God's team. Use the space below to record what you discovered.

Every Team Needs Cheers

1. We were lost in sin,
   Till God set us free.
   Thru Christ we have,
   The victory!

2. We're number one,
   In the name of the Son,
   Serving our God,
   And sharing the fun.

3. We're on the team.
   We're on the team.
   We're on the team to serve our
       Lord.

4. Put on the armor of God
   And walk in the light of His
       love.
   Through the power of the Spirit,
   We can do all things,
   Serving man and the God
       above.

2

A United Team

(Eph. 4:1–16)

Where We're Heading

Called to one team, God has provided us with different gifts. He desires for us to use our gifts for a purpose. Unfortunately, we often fail to use our gifts to do what He intends. Through Christ God offers us forgiveness when we misuse or fail to use our gifts to His glory. As the Holy Spirit strengthens our faith through the Gospel, we eagerly and willingly offer our gifts to Him in service. The team analogy offers many insights into these gifts and their purpose.

This lesson emphasizes unity and teamwork. Those concepts present a unique challenge to those working with teenagers. Youth live in a "put-down" culture. Even if they deeply care about someone they may not express it verbally. Instead, they might resort to friendly teasing and put-downs. While such actions can seem harmless on the surface, they can, in reality, work against the development of unity in God's family.

You have an important role in counteracting this tendency among teens. It is vital that you strive to recognize the value of each person in your class. Attempt on a regular basis to speak friendly and supportive words to each individual. Discourage the use of nicknames or negative comments in the classroom. Most important, model Christian behavior yourself. The way you treat the individual members of the class will have an effect.

Objectives

By the end of this session, the participants will be able to
1. rejoice in God's calling him or her through Baptism to faith and service;
2. discuss the gifts and talents that God has given them;
3. identify the purpose toward which God is working.

Materials Needed

- Bibles
- Pencils
- Copies of Student Pages 6 and 7
- A baptismal certificate
- Copies of the Student Page 3, "Who Will Make the Team?"
- Pictures of a Baptism
- Blank paper and markers for affirmation messages and slogans (optional)

Bible Study Outline: A United Team

Activity	Minutes	Materials Needed
As the Students Arrive		Student Page 1
Evaluating the Team	10	Student Page 3
Or . . .		
Corporate Raider	10	
Our Role on God's Team	20	Student Page 7, Bibles
An Affirmation Exercise	15	Bibles
Or . . .		
Affirmation Notes	15	blank paper, Bibles
Making God's Team	15	Student Page 4, Bibles
The Good News: You Still Make the Team	10	Bibles, Student Page 4
Closing Activity	5	Student Page 5

As the Students Arrive

Greet the students as they arrive. If any students are new, you will want to review the introductory materials with them. Use Student Page 1 to introduce them to Ephesians and to Paul's purpose for writing it. Stress that Paul's words of encouragement were intended to help the Ephesians in their efforts to share God's message in a difficult situation.

Have a copy of a blank baptismal certificate available for the class members to look at. You can probably obtain one from your pastor. As an alternative, you could bring your baptismal certificate or ask a class member to bring one from home. Pictures or photographs of Baptisms posted around the room would be a nice touch. You could also replay a portion of Tom Rogers' video suggested in the Introduction. Informally discuss the sacrament of Baptism. "What happens in Baptism? What are the benefits?" Ask students if they are aware of the date of their Baptism. A person's baptismal birthday is an important day in their lives. It can be celebrated in a similar way to our regular birthday. It is the day when God gave us new life through His Son.

Introductory Activity

Greet the class and then begin with a brief prayer such as the following: "Gracious Heavenly Father, bless our class today. As we study Your Word, help us to discover the important role that we play in Your kingdom. Help us also to see the role that others play, so that we might all work together in sharing Your love. Amen."

Then use either of the following activities.

Evaluating the Team

Remind class members of the activity from the previous session in which they selected a basketball team. Ask them to pretend that they have spent a week working with that team. They will now evaluate the talents of the team. Move class members into their small groups and distribute copies of Student Page 3, "Who Will Make the Team?" Allow students to review the players they selected. Also hand out Student Page 6. Encourage the students to use their imagination in evaluating the players.

After no more than 10 minutes, or when you sense that all groups have completed the assignment, call the class together. Discuss the assignment with them. "Was it easy to evaluate players? Was it harder to find positive things to say or negative ones? How would you feel about evaluating real people in the same way? Why is it more beneficial to emphasize the positive attributes of a person than the negative ones?"

Or . . .

The Corporate Raider (An Alternate Activity)

This activity requires at least 6 participants.

Divide the class into its small groups. Inform the class that each small group is the board of directors of a new corporation. The first task of each small group is to select a president. To simplify that task, choose the person in that small group who has a birthday closest to the date on which you are teaching the lesson. The first job for the president is to appoint a recruiter from his group. A young company needs talented people if it is to grow. The recruiter should be someone who can judge the talents of others.

Once the recruiter is appointed, it is his or her task to go to another small group and recruit an individual to join his or her company (team). The recruiter goes to another group and selects one person other than the president or the recruiter of the small group. Once that person is selected, the recruiter briefly interviews him or her to determine his or her qualifications. When the interview is completed, the recruiter takes the individual back to the president of his or her team. The recruit is introduced to the president and his or her strengths shared. As an example: "This is Shawn. He is a talented and good-looking guy. I think he would be a positive force on our team because he knows how to relate to other people." The president then introduces the new recruit to the company/small group, stressing the individual's positive attributes.

After each small group has selected a new recruit, call the class together. Inform the entire class that the new recruits were so successful that they have now become the president of their group. The new president is to appoint a new recruiter, and the process is repeated. The game can continue for three or more rounds.

At the conclusion call the class together and discuss the experience with them. Ask the recruits how it felt to be selected? Ask others how it felt not to be recruited? Ask recruiters if it was difficult to select someone? What qualities did they look for in a teammate?

Our Role on God's Team

Move the participants back into their small groups. Ask each group to appoint a secretary, who will record the answers for the group.

Distribute copies of Student Page 7, "Our Role on God's Team." Allow 15 minutes for the students to complete the assignment. At the end of that time call the class together. Invite groups to share their responses. Emphasize the following points.

1. We are called to keep the unity of the Spirit through the bond of peace with all those whom God has called into His family.

2. Humility, gentleness, patience, and love are possible responses.

3. Members of God's team, the church, are part of God's family through Baptism. We all share the same hope of eternal life. Our common faith motivates us to demonstrate a spirit of unity.

4. God gives His people gifts for works of service to build up the body of Christ.

5. The goal is unity in the faith and in knowledge of the Son of God, so that we may attain the whole measure of the fullness of Christ.

Before moving on, review this basic concept with the participants: God desires unity in His family so that people might serve Him and extend His kingdom." Point out that at times all people fail to use God's gifts for His purposes. God in Christ forgives us for these failures. He empowers us by His love to use our gifts to do good works that will strengthen or increase His kingdom.

People As God's Gifts

Lead your group through either of the following activities to help them recognize the gifts that God has given others.

An Affirmation Exercise

Model affirmation as you recognize each member of the group for their contribution to the class. Keep your comments positive. Say, "Bob, I really appreciate the way you always give us a new perspective," rather than "Bob, your comments are often inappropriate."

When you have affirmed the members of the class, move them into their small groups. Ask them to do the same exercise in their small group. Select someone in each group to be the first individual to receive affirmation. Do that by saying something such as this: "The person wearing the most blue listens first." The selected student will listen while each member of the group says at least one affirming thing about him or her. Encourage participants to be creative and positive. The person being affirmed should not respond. After everyone has affirmed the first individual, the person to the left takes a turn at being affirmed.

Or . . .

Affirmation Notes

As an alternative to the exercise above, divide the class into small groups and furnish each participant with a sheet of paper. Instruct them to tear the paper into pieces, one piece for each member of their small group. Direct them to write an affirming message to each individual. The messages are then delivered personally.

After no more than 10 minutes, bring your chosen activity to a close. Direct each small group to look at **Eph. 4:14–16.** Each group should read it together. Following the reading, instruct group members to develop another motivational slogan based on this section. Examples might include "Speak the truth in love," or "Anchored in Christ and surrounded by friends, I can face every storm the devil sends my way."

When all groups have completed the assignment, call the class together and ask each group to share its slogan. If tape or other material for mounting the slogans is available, place the slogans on the walls around the room.

Closing

Use one of the class cheers from Student Page 5 to end the session, or lead the students in a prayer such as this: "Thank You for the opportunity to be together today as Your people. Thank You for the many individual gifts You give this class. Help us to grow in our love and respect for each other. Amen."

Follow-Up Activities

A Churchwide Emphasis on Baptism

Share the following information. "A common practice for former generations of Christians was to frame their baptismal certificates and mount them on the walls of their bedrooms. The presence of the certificate served as a daily reminder of the Christian's membership in God's family."

Encourage students to initiate a campaign to make people more aware of their baptismal covenant. Students could

• Find out the dates of their baptisms and list those dates on a chart that can be displayed in the classroom.

• Develop posters concerning Baptism and hang them throughout the church building.

• Send congratulatory cards to parents of children who are newly baptized. The cards would recognize the Baptism of the child but also challenge parents to remember their own baptismal vow.

• Supervise the preparation of a monthly calendar that includes every church member's baptismal anniversary.

Finally, as teacher you could send cards to the students on their Baptism birthday rather than their actual birthday. Students could also celebrate that day with their friends.

Baptism: Sacrament of Belonging

The film *Baptism: Sacrament of Belonging* continues to be an effective teaching tool.

The brief film tells the story of a badly deformed Mexican boy who was orphaned as the result of a fire. The boy approaches a Catholic orphanage and appeals to the priest to allow him to enter. The priest is full of compassion but also afraid of how the other boys will react to the boy's appearance. The priest agrees to talk to the other children. He tells them of the boy's plight, and they agree to accept him. In a dramatic scene the deformed boy is brought in and introduced. There is a long silence while we view the compassionate faces of the crowd. Finally the silence is broken as one young boy steps forward and offers words of welcome, "You are my brother." The closing scene shows all the residents of the orphanage in a joyous celebration.

The film is available from Mass Media Ministries (2116 N. Charles, Baltimore, MD 21218), but it is popular enough that it might be available from a local film library as well. It would be an appropriate tool to use either as an introduction or a follow-up.

Evaluating Our Team

A good coach knows the strengths and weaknesses of every player on his or her team. In class last week you and your fellow coaches drafted six players to make up your basketball team. In the space below evaluate each of those players. Imagine that you have had the opportunity to view them in practice for one week. Try to visualize what strong points and deficiencies you might have observed, in addition to the information acquired when you drafted them.

Player	Strengths	Weaknesses
Player 1: _____		
Player 2: _____		
Player 3: _____		
Player 4: _____		
Player 5: _____		
Player 6: _____		

Ephesians, Student Page 6 © 1994 CPH

Our Role on God's Team

A Study of Ephesians 4:1–16

Ephesians 4:1–6

1. To what have you been called?

2. What characteristics can we demonstrate "to live a life worthy of the calling [we] have received?"

3. All members of the team share the same hope. What is that hope? What does this mean to individual members?

Ephesians 4:11–16

4. What is God's purpose in giving these gifts?

5. What is the ultimate goal?

3

Winning Strategies for the Team

(Eph. 4:17–5:21)

Where We're Heading

As we come to faith in Jesus and receive forgiveness and new life in the Spirit, God equips us with a Christ-like character, enabling us to live a life of discipleship. Such qualities are best described as what Christ does in us, rather than the fruits of our own effort.

Objectives

By the end of this session, the participants will be able to
1. contrast Paul's pictures in Ephesians of life with and without Christ;
2. identify ways in which God empowers their daily life;
3. give thanks for the love of God demonstrated through the sacrifice of Christ.

Materials Needed

- Bibles
- Pencils
- Copies of Student Pages 8–10 for each student
- Extra copies of Student Page 10
- Paper and marking pens

Bible Study Outline: Winning Strategies for the Team

Activity	Minutes	Materials Needed
Introductory Activity	10	"Please Start without Me" sign or magazines and newspapers, Student Page 8
Time Out for Prayer	5	
A Difficult Loss	15	Student Page 9, Bibles
Support Strategies	10	Newsprint or paper and markers
Giving Thanks	10	Student Page 10
Closing	5	

Introductory Activity

Option 1: "Please Start without Me"

This activity intends to help participants learn what life is like without leadership. You should have all your materials prepared in advance. Either carry them with you or hide them in the classroom. Write the message "Please Start without Me" on a chalkboard or a sheet of newsprint. If you are unsure of your class' ability to discipline itself in your absence, recruit another adult to monitor the room. Instruct that individual to inform the class that you have asked him or her to watch the room until you arrive. This person should make it clear that he or she is not prepared to teach.

If you do not use a person to monitor the class, make sure that you inform the others responsible for the program (Sunday school superintendent, etc.) of your plans.

Give your class about 10 minutes to work independently. When you arrive in the classroom, act surprised that they have not begun the session. If they have attempted to begin, congratulate them on their effort and inquire on the progress they have made.

Then quiz them on the experience using the following questions. "Why didn't you begin without me?" (They had no materials. They didn't know what to do.) "In my absence, who was the leader?" (Possibly nobody; maybe one of the students. Don't let them place any responsibility on the other adult, who was only there to monitor.) "Could you function this way on a regular basis? Could regular school classrooms function this way? What roles do leaders play, anyway?" (Answers will vary, but the point is that leadership is important and necessary. Leaders play key roles in helping a group to function and accomplish its purpose.) Conclude this portion of the session by reviewing Paul's desire that the Ephesians make Christ their leader **(Eph. 4:1–6)** and be imitators of Him **(Eph. 5:1)**.

Option 2: A Team without a Leader

As the students arrive, have available recent newspapers and magazines with articles dealing with various kinds of leadership. Such articles might deal with athletic coaches, government officials, or parents. Place the articles on tables around the room or post them on the walls. Direct the students to the articles as they enter the room. Encourage them to read the articles to discover a characteristic of leadership. Each student should then use a marker to write and/or illustrate that characteristic on a large sheet of newsprint, creating a leadership mural.

Call the class together around the leadership mural. Review the characteristics listed. Invite students to suggest others. Keep the mural posted in the room throughout the session as a reminder of the qualities needed for leadership.

Now distribute copies of Student Page 8, "A Team without a Leader." Have the students work in small groups as in the previous sessions. Or have them complete the activity independently.

33

After five minutes call the class together. Ask them to share their responses. Responses may include the following: *country*, no one to enforce laws or to make major decisions; *athletic team*, no one to develop strategies or determine players' positions; *family*, no one to set rules and to maintain schedule; *church*, no one to make major decisions.

Time Out for Prayer

Ask for a volunteer to lead in an opening prayer or pray as follows: "Dear Father, thank You for being our God and our Leader. We are grateful that we can look to You for guidance and comfort. We are thankful too that You have given us Jesus as our Savior and Model of servanthood. Work through Your Word today to make us more dedicated followers of Him. In Jesus' name. Amen."

A Difficult Loss

This portion of the lesson continues the concept of the basketball team from previous sessions. It challenges participants to apply the principles of discipleship.

Divide the class into small groups. Distribute Student Page 9, "A Difficult Loss." Have a volunteer read the story aloud. A second volunteer could read **Eph. 4:29–5:2.** Each individual should write a response to share with their group, reflecting what he or she would say to team members.

Ask each group to evaluate the individual responses and choose the one they think might work best. When they have done so, invite each group to share their choice.

Then ask the following questions of the class. "Is it easy to control your emotions in unfair situations? What responsibility does the coach or the Christian players on the team have in such a situation? Is it easy or hard for you to exhibit Christian behavior in such situations? Do you think Paul is realistic in his instructions to the Ephesians?" Encourage students to wrestle with the questions. Accept all answers, but ask for the reasoning behind each response.

Say, "At times it may be difficult, or seem impossible to control your temper when you are treated unfairly. Our sinful nature might urge us to 'get even'. But thanks be to God! While we were still His enemies, separated from Him because of our sin, God did not get even with us. Instead, He did something miraculous for us." Read, or have a volunteer read, how God dealt with us, His enemies **(Rom. 5:6–8).** Say, "God's great love for us, the love that caused Him to send His only Son to earth to suffer and die for us, enables us to love others, even those who hurt us." Reread **Eph. 4:29, 31–5:2.** Begin each verse with the words, "God's love for us in Jesus enables us to—"

Support Strategies

Say, "Christians face many difficult situations in life. God's expecta-

34

tions of us are very high. Through Christ He forgives repentant sinners for their failures. He also supports us through His Spirit as we seek to do His will. The question is, how does that happen?"

Direct the students back to their small groups. Challenge them to brainstorm ways they can support and encourage each other in Christ-like responses to difficult situations. Furnish each group with a sheet of newsprint and marking pens. Ask them to record their ideas so that they can share them with the entire class. Allow about 10 minutes for the groups to complete the assignment. At the end of that time, invite each group to share what it has written. Typical responses might be Bible study, prayer, and having Christian friends.

Giving Thanks

Distribute copies of Student Page 10, "Giving Thanks." After making sure every participant has a pencil or pen, ask them to complete the acrostic. A sample acrostic follows:

Thankful
Hearts
Always
Ack **N**owledge
Kindness
Your
L **O**rd
Unleashes

Allow about five minutes for the students to work independently. Then have each student share their work with a partner. Give each pair an additional copy of Student Page 10. Ask them to use their combined resources to write one more acrostic. Then invite partners to share their work with the class.

Closing

Ask for a volunteer to read **Eph. 5:19–20** aloud to the class. Encourage other class members to follow along in their Bibles.

Close the session with a prayer such as the following: "Loving Father, thank You for the gift of Your Son, Jesus Christ, as our Savior. Through the power of Your Spirit enable us to be your faithful servants. Assure us of Your forgiveness when we fail and of Your promise to give us the strength and courage to try again and again. Amen."

Follow-Up Activities

Teen Cheers

One way to close the session is to use one of the printed cheers found on Student Page 5. Encourage students to develop additional cheers of their own.

Or . . . .

Praise Songs

Using **Eph. 5:19–20** as a basis, encourage the students to write new songs of praise. As examples of such songs, direct them to **Psalm 100** or **103.** Rather than using a traditional religious melody, why not encourage the students to use familiar TV theme songs as possible melodies.

Or . . . .

Practice, Practice, Practice

Developing and supporting a Christian lifestyle is an ongoing task. Perhaps this study could be the starting point for a small group ministry at the local high schools where your students attend. While a local high school cannot support such a ministry by providing staff or publicity, they can provide space, as they do for other clubs, if it is requested. As an alternative, a home or fast-food restaurant close to the campus might be a possible site. Use class members who possess leadership skills to assist as a small-group leader. Provide them resources and training.

A Team without a Leader

Life without a leader can be difficult. Most of life's situations call for someone to step forward and lead. How could the lack of leadership affect each of the following?

- **A country**

- **An athletic team**

- **A family**

- **A church**

A Difficult Loss

Imagine you are the coach. Your team was just starting to take shape. After three games you have two victories and a defeat. Your fourth game is against one of your archrivals on their court. You anticipate a close game. The referees seem to be partial to the other team. Several close calls go against you. As a result your best player fouls out with 5 minutes left. The game becomes lop-sided from that point on. You lose by 10 points.

During the game your opponent's fans cheer loudly for their team. As the game becomes more intense they become rude and obnoxious. Several of their fans sitting behind your bench resort to name-calling and making fun of your players. When the game ends you desire to leave as quickly as possible. You still try to greet your opponents and their coach to congratulate them on the victory. Instead of accepting your best wishes, they remark, "We're so out of your league the game should have never been close."

You go to the locker room angry. When you get there you discover a couple of your players vandalizing the room. When you ask them to stop they remark, "After that game, they deserve it." While you still desire to depart quickly, you feel a need to talk to your team. Use the space below to write what you would say.

Before you begin, read **Ephesians 4:29–5:2.**

Giving Thanks

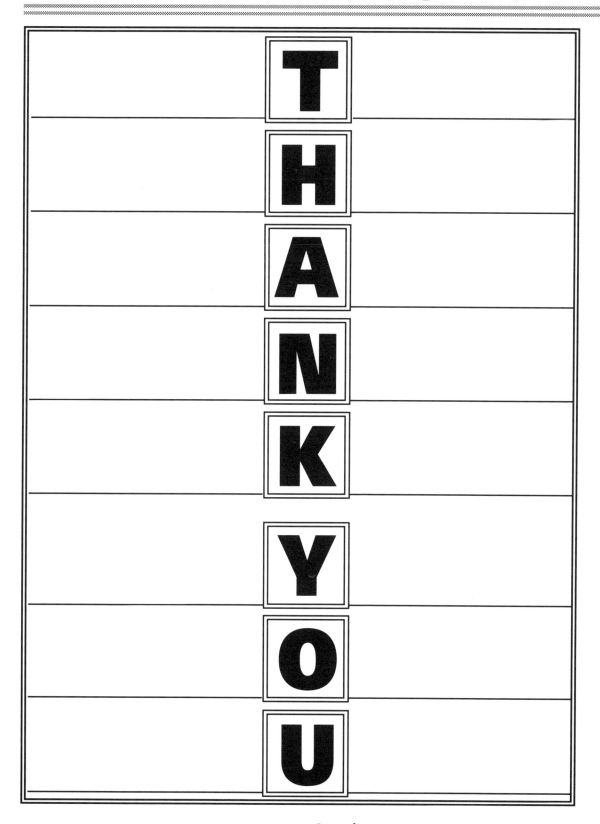

Ephesians, Student Page 10

Equipped for Victory

(Eph. 6:10–24)

Where We're Heading

The victory we have in Jesus' death and resurrection is unlike any earthly victory we may experience. Earthly victories are few and fleeting. Our victory in Christ is eternal. Earthly victories have little power. Through Christ, by God's grace, we are equipped in a powerful way to work together to build His kingdom. The day-to-day challenges of life may overwhelm us at times. Through the power of the Spirit, God enables us to meet those challenges.

Objectives

By the end of this session, the participants will be able to
1. recognize the "armor of God" as a gracious gift;
2. identify circumstances in their lives where the "armor" is of benefit;
3. commit themselves to sharing "the mystery of the Gospel" with God's help.

Materials Needed

- Bibles
- Pencils
- Copies of Student Pages 11–13 for each student
- Aluminum foil and newspaper (optional)
- Plain paper

Bible Study Outline: Equipped for Victory

Activity	Minutes	Materials Needed
Introduction	5	Newspapers and magazines, or other resources
The Armor of God	15	Student Page 11, newspaper, foil, and other craft (optional)
It's a Long Season	20	Student Page 12, chalkboard and chalk or newsprint and markers, paper
Sharing the Joy	15	Student Page 13
Closing	5	Student Page 5 (optional)

As the Students Arrive

Greet students as they arrive. Since this is the last session in this study you will want to evaluate your teaching efforts. You could begin the evaluation at this time. Complete it at the end of the session. Ask participants questions such as, "What have you learned from this study? What principles presented were most applicable to your situation right now? Which activities were the most fun? What would you do to make future session more valuable?" Record the answers for future planning.

Locate newspaper or magazine articles that feature leaders who model Christian values—athletes, political figures, and entertainers. A Fellowship of Christian Athletes chapter may have this information. Have information available for students to look at informally prior to class.

Introduction

Lead the class in an opening prayer such as the following: "Gracious Heavenly Father, we thank You for the gift of Your Word and for the opportunities You have given us to study it in these sessions. Bless our study today. Help us in all things to seek ways that we can serve others more fully in Your name. Amen."

Say, "This study will conclude our look at Paul's letter to the Ephesians. Paul closes the letter by reminding the Ephesians, and us, of the tools that God has given us to carry out His work. We will review those tools and discover practical ways to use them."

The Armor of God

Distribute copies of Student Page 11, "The Armor of God." Instruct the students to read **Eph. 6:10–18** individually. Then have them fill in the blanks next to the verses, according to the instructions on the page. Answers include the following: **v. 14**—belt of truth, breastplate of righteousness; **v. 15**—ready feet; **v. 16**—shield of faith; **v. 17**—helmet of salvation and sword of the spirit.

After students have identified the six items of spiritual armor have them equip the teen on the student page with the various items listed. Encourage creativity. For instance, Paul no doubt modeled his "armor" after the Roman centurions with whom he was familiar. The students might choose a contemporary model such as a football player, modern soldier, or construction worker.

An active alternative to drawing the armor would be to have the students construct their own. Divide the class into groups of three. Provide each group with simple, disposable materials such as newspaper and aluminum foil. Ask each group to elect someone to equip with armor. A simple headpiece could be made of paper. Use foil to construct a shield and sword. Allow 10–15 minutes for each group to complete the assignment.

Have a "fashion show" to allow each group to share what they have developed.

It's a Long Season

Remind the class of the basketball team analogy used in previous sessions. Distribute Student Page 12, "It's a Long Season." It presents seven different situations team members could find themselves in.

On a chalkboard or sheet of newsprint write the following instructions:

"How would you as a Christian respond to this situation?"

1. Write out your response in a complete paragraph.

2. Use our previous studies in Ephesians to help you formulate your answer.

3. Include quotations from the Bible when possible.

There are a number of ways to assign this to the class.

• If you have a small class, you could allow each participant to select one or two of the situations.

• Students could work in pairs.

• You could assign each situation to a different small group of three to five students.

Provide each participant or group with one sheet of blank paper for each situation they will complete. Allow the students about 10 minutes to complete the assignment.

When most are nearly done, invite participants, pairs, or small groups to share their responses. After listening to a report ask, "How many agree with the prepared response?" Invite those who disagree to make suggestions. Ask each group to support their responses using verses from Ephesians. Allow others to offer other supporting Scripture passages. Also ask, "How difficult would it be to do the Christ-like thing in this situation?"

The responses to this activity will vary. Allow the students to discuss each situation freely. Ask, "What happens when we make unwise decisions—decisions contrary to God's will for our lives?" Answers may include suffer consequences, get hurt, or lose respect for ourself. Then say, "When you experience guilt over your sinful failures, remember God invites you through Christ to receive complete forgiveness. His love for you strengthens and empowers you to make wise decisions."

Sharing the Joy

Remind the class that Paul ends the letter with some very personal thoughts. His comments provide us with insight into his philosophy of life and guidelines for our personal lives of discipleship.

Distribute copies of Student Page 13, "Sharing the Joy." Form small groups to work together on this closing project. Each group should appoint someone to read the verses and someone to record the responses. Give the small groups 10 minutes to complete the task.

Call the class together. Ask for volunteers to share their guidelines. Possible responses: "Pray constantly for each other" or "Do God's will fearlessly." If any participants have had trouble completing the assignment, suggest that they listen to the ideas shared by their classmates.

Encourage the students to take this page home as a reminder of the study and their commitment to a life of discipleship in Jesus' name.

Closing

Close with a prayer such as the following: "Gracious Father, we thank You for the opportunity to study Your Word. Now we ask that You help us to apply Your Word to our lives. We want to be Your people in ministry. Provide us with a fuller measure of Your Spirit that we might do that. Forgive us when we fail. Give us the power to grow in our ministry to You. In Your Son's name we pray. Amen."

You could also conclude the lesson with one of the cheers (Student Page 5).

Follow-Up Activities

A Class Mission Statement

Develop a class mission statement. A typical mission statement might read, "We are a caring group of young Christians who have come together to grow in God's Word, pray for each other, and encourage one another to be fearless disciples as we share the love of Jesus with those around us through our words and actions."

Ask the class to consider ways that Paul's letter to the Ephesians has affected their mission statement.

Where Does My Armor Need Work?

Refer the class back to the "Armor of God" activity. On a chalkboard or sheet of newsprint again list the pieces of armor. Distribute blank paper to the students. Ask them to copy the list. Request that each participant evaluate themselves in each area using questions such as, "In what shape is your belt of truth? How strong is your shield of faith? How strong is your sword of the Spirit?

Encourage class members to seek ways to grow in those areas where they are spiritually deficient. Emphasize that the Holy Spirit strengthens our faith through His Word and Sacraments. Ask, "What kind of goals do you have for the future?"

Evaluation

You may have begun an evaluation process informally during the presession. Continue that process now. Such evaluation is a valuable part of every educational experience.

For a simple evaluation, distribute a blank paper to all participants. Request that in their own words they respond to the following questions:

1. What is the most significant thing you learned in this study of Ephesians?

2. What activities were the most enjoyable?

3. What would you do to make future sessions more effective and enjoyable?

The Armor of God

In **Ephesians 6:10–18,** Paul identifies the spiritual armor that God provides His disciples. List the specific pieces of armor he mentions in the blanks next to the proper verses below.

verse 14

_____

_____

verse 15

_____

verse 16

_____

verse 17

_____

_____

What might be a contemporary set of protective clothing? Draw each of the items listed above on the figure outline . Be as creative as you wish.

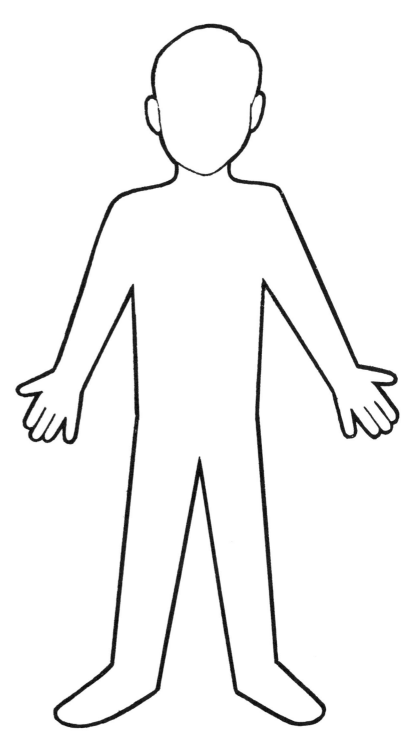

A Long Season: Some Tough Decisions

You are a member of a basketball team. As the season progresses you are faced with some difficult decisions. Some of the situations are personal, others involve members of your team. Use **Ephesians 6:10–18** to assist you in your reaction. In developing your response, quote from Ephesians or other books of the Bible if possible. Consider parts of armor that could be helpful.

1. Members of your team always join in prayer in the locker room before and after each game. Participation is voluntary. A parent who is not a Christian has asked the coach to stop the practice. What will you do?

2. Two players on your team have a major disagreement over a dating relationship. One girl threatens to ignore the other on the court by not passing the ball to her. The second girl is one of the best players. What will you do?

3. In the middle of the season a close friend of yours from your church youth group is diagnosed as having AIDS. You find it hard to concentrate on basketball. It's affecting your performance. What will you do?

A Long Season: Some Tough Decisions—Continued

4. A coach from an opposing team accuses your coach of running up the score and using unfair tactics. He is telling other teams to avoid playing your team. You know his charges are untrue. What will you do?

5. A college recruiter offers you and your parents a weekend at a resort near their campus. He tells you that you are not obligated to visit the campus, but you suspect that is part of the deal. You know such arrangements are illegal. What will you do?

6. You have suspected that one of your teammates and her/his boyfriend/girlfriend are sexually active. While out shopping you observe them purchasing condoms. They did not see you. You have always considered the persons involved to be your friends. What will you do?

7. As the season progresses both you and your team get better. At the close of the season you are selected for the all-star team. A local newspaper wants to feature you in a major article. What will you do?

Ephesians, Student Page 12B

Sharing the Joy

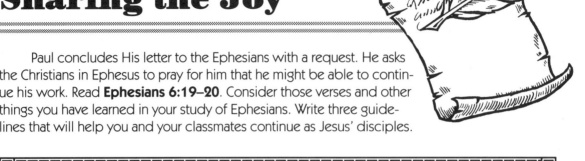

Paul concludes His letter to the Ephesians with a request. He asks the Christians in Ephesus to pray for him that he might be able to continue his work. Read **Ephesians 6:19–20**. Consider those verses and other things you have learned in your study of Ephesians. Write three guidelines that will help you and your classmates continue as Jesus' disciples.

Guideline 1

Guideline 2

Guideline 3